How to win in a pandemic crisis

By: Alfredo Chu

Jan 2021

January 2021

Alfredo Chu has an MBA from Tulane University (United States) and a master's degree in global business administration (PUCP-Centrum - World), he has a bachelor's degree in Electronic Engineering from Ricardo Palma University (World), He has several technological specializations applied in various industries such as mining and energy in countries such as the United States, Germany, World, Switzerland, Sweden, Brazil, Chile and South Africa.

Previously, he served as Director of Mining and Digital for General Electric in LATAM for 5 years. He was Commercial Director of ABB in the Energy System (PS) division for 4 years; where he achieved the largest and most profitable contract for the region, including the introduction of a financial model never made by the company and that later became the standard for countries like Brazil and Switzerland. He has held various management positions for Siemens Germany for 10 years and achieved hundreds of deals and profitable deals worth tens of millions of dollars. He is currently a shareholder and founding partner of Novica.com, which is based in the United States, California, with National Geographic as a partner with offices in World, Mexico, Brazil, India, Thailand, Ghana, Bali and Java and Central America.

Currently he is a founding partner of three companies, that has been multiplied the sales in 1882% with his team from 2018 to 2019.

In 2020 due to the pandemic, sales fell 80% due to a strategic decision, I will explain it to you because the net profit only fell by

4%. How can be achieved? Well, there is what we call capital strategy, focus and strawberry shortcake.

The holding company currently has a market valuation carried out by third parties for a value of $ 10,334,429.01 Million Dollars. The model used for the FCF is derived from the Gordon & Shapiro three-stage model with a discount rate of 9%, with a dividend policy of 20%, for which 80% of the profits will be capitalized annually.

As an interesting fact, at least 5 national and international investors have tried to buy part of our company before and during the pandemic, due to the high degree of Disruption and innovation and especially because of the value of the company share that we estimate will be capitalized drastically right now during the pandemic, for good strategic decisions and for entering high-growth sectors and great prospects at the national and global level. We have not sold because we are waiting for the best moment of capitalization.

This book is very compressed because we will forget about fancy terms used in many top ivy league universities with many professors who have never worked in a real work and have to use his own cash to payroll.

This book is for the real world using the best practices and we will learn from the best managers also.

We will teach you the best practices in the world so that you can apply them in your business now! You will also learn from the bankruptcy of prominent international companies for not using common sense and dealing with their emotions.

The best investor in the world is Warren Buffett, we all make mistakes, but it is better to learn from the mistakes that others made.

There are sectors that you surely have not seen and they are there ready to take them

We will show them to you.

How to make your company prosper in the Full Covid19 Pandemic

Index

Chapter 1. Strategic Plan

    1.1 Concept

    1.2 How to develop a strategic plan

Chapter 2. Business Opportunities

    2.1 Sale of products

    2.2 Sale of Services

    2.3 Innovation and disruptive models

Chapter 3. Organization and Human Resources

    3.1 Organization chart

    3.2 The Winning Team

    3.3 Evaluation of your team

Chapter 4. Funding Sources

    4.1 Various sources of financing

Chapter 5. Finance

    5.1 How to read and understand a Financial Statement

5.2 Key indicators

5.3 The accounting trap

5.4 Why companies go bankrupt

5.5 Because companies are successful and sustainable

Chapter 1. Strategic Plan

The ideal for any company or entrepreneur is to take the largest and fastest growing market, however, we must take into account the following, which I will explain in the next point: Concept 1.1

1.1 Concept

What is a strategic plan and what is the only reason you need to have a strategy?

I have asked this question to hundreds of managers, entrepreneurs and more than 80% have a tangled idea, they confuse what is a vision, an objective, what a mission is and end up confusing everything, that is, they are not clear why a strategy it is necessary.

As an anecdote Personally throughout my career of more than 25 years in very large companies, you will be surprised that many C-Level Managers (that is the name for high-level managers) or even highly ranked functional managers and employees from many countries where I have worked, in Europe such as Germany, Switzerland, Finland, USA, etc. They have a confusion of the concept and this is crucial to be very clear, for this I will rely on two (2) graphics and a small fiction, thus, you are not going to never forget.

Imagine that you are on a flight and one of the turbines collapses, the pilot has no choice but to make a forced landing, however it does not go well and they fall on a desert island and of the 300 passengers only you and a beautiful woman are save, you will not be rescued and will remain on the island until death.

What will happen between you and the woman?

Ohhhh, they will eventually become friends and the inevitable will happen. They will be like Adam and Eve on the desert island. It is not like this? Will you need to use a sophisticated strategy to conquer the beautiful woman? Or you will enjoy her attention for as long as possible? You will have a Monopoly on their needs and their thoughts for the rest of the days until death do them part.

Your strategy to conquer the beautiful woman will not have to be so sophisticated, it will come to you alone because it has no other option, loneliness would kill her with boredom, now if you want to rush things, you will be more proactive, and you will do "productive" things. to conquer it in the shortest time possible, that is, you will increase your efficiency.

But strategy nothing, there is only one way to get there and it is a direct line.

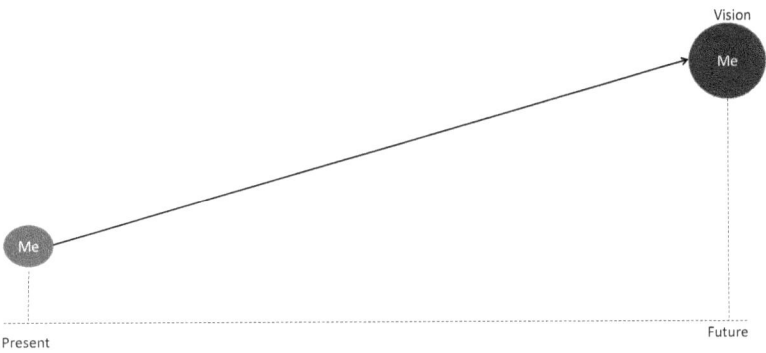

But what if the beautiful woman, you, and several men on the plane also survive? The answer is obvious, right? I don't need to explain it to you.

So remember, the only reason a strategy is required is because you have competitors.

Where most companies fail is that they do not know the needs of their client (Women) and secondly they do not know the competition.

We will try to solve it in chapter 1.2 how to develop a strategic plan

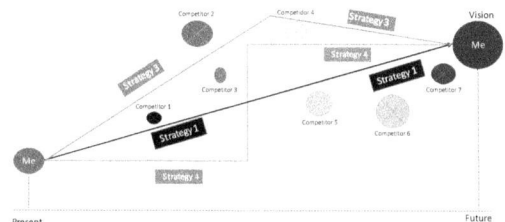

Remember, the present is today and the future is the vision, the paths you use to achieve your vision depend on you from your company and the most important thing to clearly define your vision.

A vision that does not have a number and a year is a dream, you must place two very important things in your vision.

When and How Much

What part of the market do you want to be yours and in what time will you achieve it.

For this you can do many things that are always ethical and allowed within the rules of the environmental game.

1.2 How to develop a strategic plan

Developing a strategic plan is not as complicated as it is taught in Harvard or other Ivy league business schools, I will tell you that 80% of what you will learn there you already know, it is all common sense.

I will teach you how to do it in three (3) simple steps, you need data.

 I. Target Market
 II. Competition Analysis
 III. Market Share

I.   Target Market (a lot of info are in internet at free cost)

<u>Imagine you are a motor manufacturer however this apply for whatever product you want to sell</u>

I will collect info here to see the total market to have the big picture

https://www.fortunebusinessinsights.com/industry-reports/electric-motor-market-100752

See the info below: the market is growing at CAGR 5.7% annually
By 2026 = USD 167.03 Billion (Market is Large)

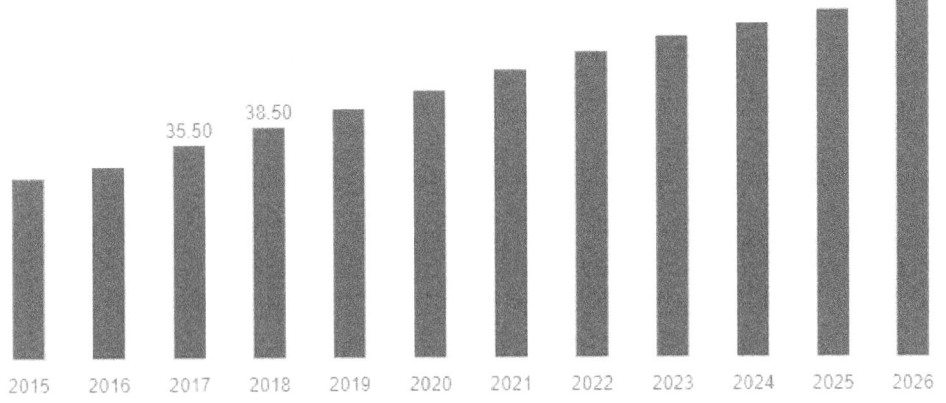

Asia-Pacific Electric Motor Market Size, 2015-2026 (USD Billion)

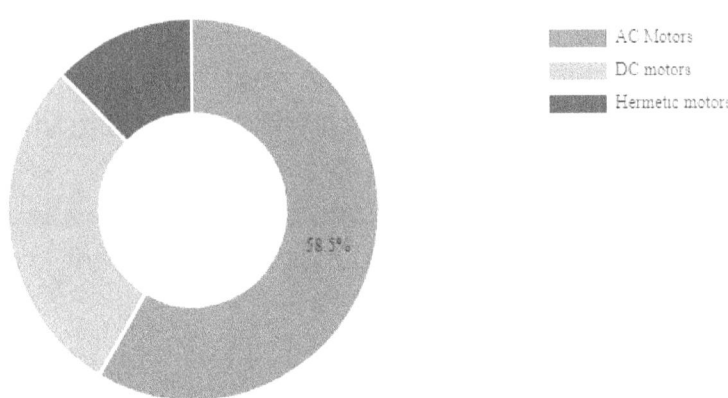

Global Electric Motor Market Share, By Motor Type, 2018

Competitors list

List Of Key Companies Profiled:

- ABB
- AMETEK
- Johnson Electric
- Siemens
- Rockwell Automation
- GE
- Nidec Motor Corporation
- WEG
- Toshiba Corporation
- Hitachi
- Mitsubishi Heavy Industries
- TECO-Westinghouse Motor Company
- Arc Systems Inc.
- DENSO
- Regal Beloit Corporation

More Data: If you are interested in a particular competitor, enter data sources where you can find how much it sells in the internal and external market, each country has information on imports and exports.

Competitors Financial Situation is very important, for example ABB is the leader, we will analyze it.

Use Yahoo Finance:

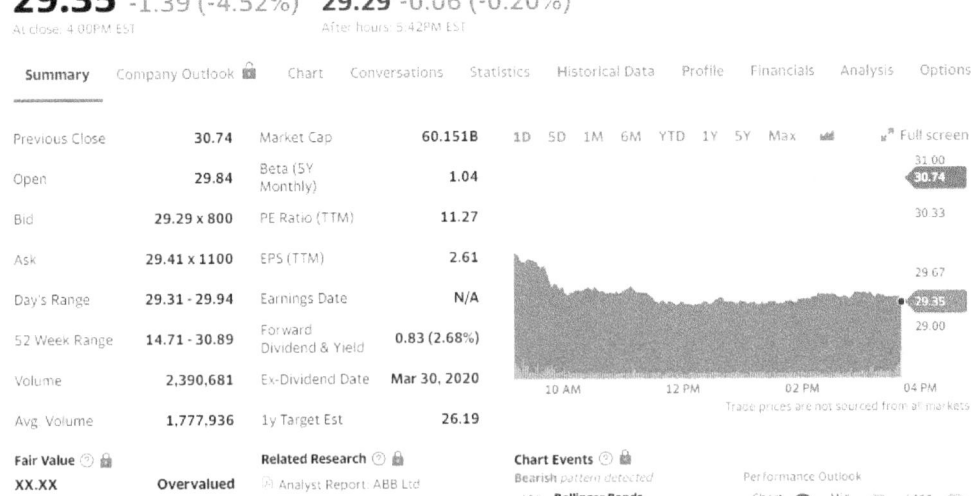

People Think the company stock is overvalued! Not always is true. Secondary market not always reflect the company reality.

You need to look its financial statement

Breakdown	TTM	12/31/2019	12/31/2018	12/31/2017
> Total Revenue	26.020.000	27.978.000	27.662.000	34.312.000
Cost of Revenue	18.082.000	19.072.000	19.118.000	24.046.000
Gross Profit	7.938.000	8.906.000	8.544.000	10.266.000
> Operating Expense	5.641.000	6.645.000	6.442.000	6.972.000
Operating Income	2.297.000	2.261.000	2.102.000	3.294.000

Look ABB is revenues stable 18/19, the operating income looks good It means Efficiency and well-managed company.

I particularly like to see the cash generation this is a more powerful indicator.

Cash Flow

All numbers in thousands

Get access to 40+ years of historical data with Yahoo Finance Premium. Learn more

Breakdown	TTM	12/31/2019	12/31/2018	12/31/2017
> Operating Cash Flow	2,422,000	2,325,000	2,924,000	3,799,000
> Investing Cash Flow	3,650,000	815,000	-3,085,000	1,450,000
> Financing Cash Flow	-4,291,000	-1,383,000	-789,000	-1,735,000
> End Cash Position	4,360,000	3,544,000	3,445,000	4,526,000
Income Tax Paid Supplemental Data	925,000	1,005,000	1,026,000	894,000
Interest Paid Supplemental Data	207,000	284,000	243,000	205,000
Capital Expenditure	-666,000	-762,000	-772,000	-949,000
Issuance of Capital Stock	393,000	10,000	42,000	163,000
Issuance of Debt	695,000	2,570,000	1,914,000	1,128,000
Repayment of Debt	-807,000	-2,156,000	-830,000	-1,007,000
Repurchase of Capital Stock	-1,270,000	0	-250,000	-251,000
Free Cash Flow	1,756,000	1,563,000	2,152,000	2,850,000

The operating cash flow is going down three consecutive years, the same for the Free Cash Flow. This is interesting Why?

Definitely with this simple analysis I am more than sure that the C-level people are pushing the sales people for improving the networking capital, it means, they need to sell stuff with cash in advance and with short credit. Look You just found a weakness in this company.

If your business can offer cashless credit up front, you can take a slice out of its market.

Always read your competitor's quarterly report to see the next move, don't forget to do it.

Annual report
2019

You should read their annual report and identify in which direction the company is going with respect to engines, if they have bought a company, sold or will make a move, if you have more time and it is published you can see if their engine area is growing or decreasing.

However, the hardest data is the amount of engines that are selling in your market and that you should be able to obtain from customs, almost all countries have a database available.

You should do the same exercise with at least your 5 main customers, they are losing money, how are their stocks, how many

Motors are they buying and from whom, the same information is available in the customs database, or you can talk with the company buyer in % they can disclosed this info for you.

With all this info, Market, Competition and Customer you can build a strategic plan.

You must identify weaknesses and strengths of your competitor and what your client needs, as simple as that. The most difficult thing is to get the data, then when you have an interesting story you can structure a path, a strategy to hit hard.

Place a couple of collaborators to get all the information and once they have it, deliver that information to your champions and they will put together the strategic plan for you.

Remember this, which is a confusion for many.

- Vision: Where I want to go and when.
- Strategy: The path we are going to choose.
- Mission: It is what your company does.
- Objective: Are the little steps you are taking to fulfill your vision.

There is no perfect method to develop a strategic plan, but what does exist is data and people smarter than you, use that to your advantage, remember only 20% of companies do it well. If you gather your champions in a couple of months they could give you a very good surprise!

Chapter 2. Business Opportunities

2.1 Sale of products

There are 2 ways to sell products in the World

I. Local distributor. - You get a client and you buy the product in the local market from a supplier, your margin will be lower and your risk will also be lower, since the product is already Nationalized. You just have to negotiate the payment method. Ideally, the client gives you an advance, which is not easy in a first sale, you will have to have at least 3 or 4 operations with your client to access it.

The same goes for the Local Provider. No serious local supplier will deliver the merchandise to you if you don't pay 100% for it. (I'll show you later how this will affect your cash flow with various scenarios.)

II. Importer. - You get a client and you buy the product in the international market, your margin will be higher and your risk will also be higher since the product will have to be imported. You just have to negotiate the payment method. Ideally, the client gives you an advance, which is not easy in a first sale, you will have to have at least 3 or 4 operations with your client for your client to access.

The same happens with the International Provider. No serious international supplier will deliver the merchandise to you if you don't pay 100% for it. (I'll show you later how this will affect your cash flow with various scenarios.)

2.2 Sale of Services

Services are the most profitable and least risky businesses from a financial point of view, their gross margin can be 40 to 50% per operation. The services are HH (Men Hours) For highly specialized niches, the rate can range between USD 500 and USD 1500 per day. The key is to have the right staff who are highly qualified, I do not recommend that you provide the services that most do because you will enter a price war and most likely you will not make money. The most daring and intelligent is to do few services, but very specialized where competition is scarce.

2.3 Innovation and disruptive models

In the world there is a great space for innovation and disruptive models. When we refer to Innovation, it may be the creation of a product that is necessary in the market but does not yet exist, or it is too expensive for the customer to buy it abroad. Here comes the ingenuity, as you will have appreciated in the previous sheets, the market is very large and do not underestimate the capacity of the workforce in your country.

Even in other countries, for example, there is a huge number of immigrants who are over-qualified and their labor cost is affordable.

The same happens with the labor force in Eastern European countries like Ukraine, Czechoslovakia just to name a few countries, the same happens with the workforce in India and China, agreements can be reached so that they manufacture what you need according to the analysis you have made of the market.

Chapter 3. Organization and Human Resources

3.1 Organization chart

The objective of having an organization chart is to be able to reflect how your company will be organized to achieve the vision that you have set for yourself, it must be structured in such a way that the tasks of each member of your team are easy to understand without ambiguity.

There are two types of organization charts:

A. Vertical organization charts
B. Matrix organization charts

Vertical org charts are for companies that keep top management at the top and where team members report from the bottom up. I will show you with an example.

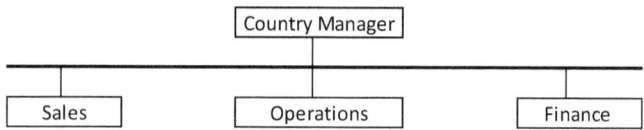

Matrix org charts are for companies that keep top management at the top and team members report from the bottom up, but also report to other management in a functional way. This type of organization charts are used in large or transnational companies. I will show you with an example

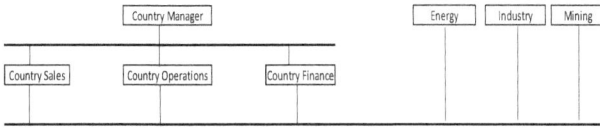

3.2 The winning team

It is companies with winning teams that make the number of their employees exceed the statistic of a rule that is 10%, 80%, 5%, 5%. What does this mean?

There are many business administration studies that agree that there are 5% of employees who are the cracks! They are like the Leonel Messi of a company. Then there is the 80% who are the ones who do their job, but they are not Messi, we call them the ants do the hard work, but they do not stand out, your goal, as a manager or entrepreneur is that in this group of 80% you can empower, at least 5% more of them and turn them into cracks!

Finally, there is a group of 5% that whatever you do will not give you results and you will have to let them go, finally there are the 5% that are the most complicated.

I will show you two (2) practical ways to identify them.

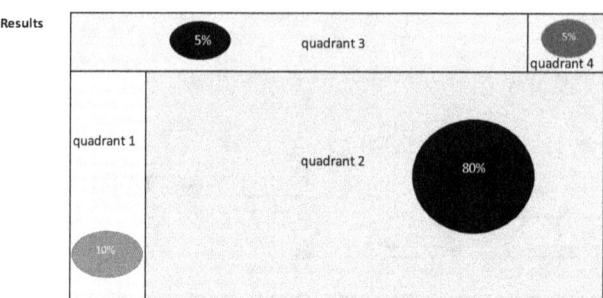

This is the classic team in all companies.

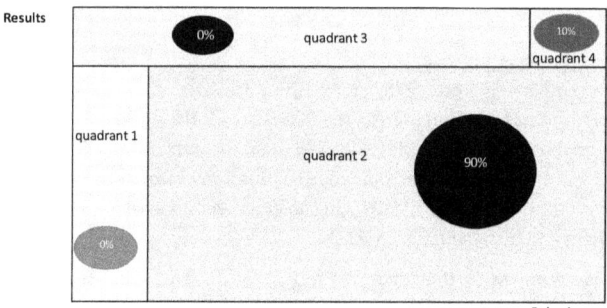

This is the winning team

You must quickly identify the employees in quadrant 1 and 3 and let them go.

Chapter 4. Funding Sources

4.1 Shareholders

If you already have a clear idea of the business, prepare 5 to 7 strong sheets and look for friends who want to associate with you, in my experience having 2 shareholders as partners is not a bad idea, they can have 33.33% each and make contributions of capital. Creating a company is not complicated at all, in two to three weeks you will have your company created with a minimum investment, there are companies that are dedicated to forming companies, you just have to go and sign, it is very simple.

The crucial thing is to choose your partners well, who not only provide financial capital, but also provide human capital (business knowledge), it can be a former co-worker, a family member, in whom you have absolute confidence. More than 3 shareholders at the beginning of the start-up of the company is ok, then you can expand if you want to get more capital.

4.2 Mortgage guarantee.

If you have a business that you think will be a success and you have already thought about it very well, you can risk your house as collateral, that will allow the bank to finance you possibly up to 50% of the value of your house. However, you must demonstrate to the bank that the income generation of your business is credible.

The other way is to obtain a personal loan (without involving the company, that is called a personal loan with a mortgage guarantee, the complicated thing about this scheme is that you must also show the bank that you as a natural person have a way to pay the installments, they will ask you pay stubs (the last 3) and affidavits of your assets.

This scheme works well when you work in a company and receive income from the 4th or 5th category on a regular basis and you already want to become independent.

4.3 Guarantor

If you are lucky enough to have a family member or a very close friend who trusts in your venture, and this person has resources, they can be the guarantor of your loan, this scheme is also widely used, but that does not oblige you to prove to the bank that your business or you can personally assume the loan payment.

4.4 State funds.

Depending on the country you are in, almost all developed and emerging countries provide funds for innovation. From USD 100,000 to 1 million. The greener, cleaner and more sustainable your invention is, the more likely it is to get funding.

4.5 European and Asian funds.

There are at least half a dozen companies that finance sustainable projects, NGOs, venture capital funds, I will not go into greater detail in this chapter, because it will totally depend on the line of business in which your company is dedicated, however, the more ecological is your company and has an impact of improvement in the reduction of greenhouse gases, poverty reduction, health improvement issues, nutrition, you will have good opportunities. Your business plan is key. You will need the help of a specialist to structure your plan, because funding ranges from $ 1 million upwards and we must demonstrate double-digit growth rates annually.

Chapter 5. Finance

5.1 How to read and understand a financial statement

Contrary to what many people think, it is not necessary to be a financial guru to read and understand a financial statement, if you develop a clinical eye and understand the line of business well, you can check in 2 hours if the company is good, regular or is on the way to bankruptcy.

If you are going to read the financial statements of your company, I advise you to be trained with someone who has a lot of experience and has read hundreds (Financial Statements), he will teach you where to look.

Probably with 4 hours of training you will be more or less prepared. There is a saying in Finance, accountants are good at recording accounting items, but few people understand whether business is doing well or poorly. That said, I'm not telling you to fire your accountant, but you, as the owner of your business, have to understand the finances, the accountant has to answer all of your questions. Do not be alarmed that there are qualified people who can help you, it is all a matter of training.

5.2 Key indicators

There are many indicators, but you should not get very dizzy you should see this:

- Sales
- Costs
- Gross margin
- Selling expenses
- Cash Flow
- Working Capital

5.3 The accounting trap

Here comes the interesting part. I say it like this: if everything you buy and sell is done in the same act, that is, for example, today you bought a bicycle for USD 500 and you sold it for USD 700 and you did it all in a single act on the same day, you paid the supplier the USD 500 and the same day your client paid you the USD 700, so their accounting will reflect a sale of USD 700, a cost of USD 500 and a profit of USD 200, understood?

In the income statement you will have a gross profit of USD 200 And in your cash flow you will have as Cash USD 200.

Also, your balance will reflect that you have $ 0 of accounts payable and $ 0 of accounts receivable.

The question is? How simple are the transactions? Not really.

What happens in practice is something very different, I'll take the same example. You buy the bicycle from your supplier for USD 500 but since he is your friend and you always buy from him, you advance him USD 300 and the rest USD 200 after 7 days.

As you are desperate to sell and you already paid USD 300 that came out of your cash, you agree to sell the bike for USD 700 with a 30-day invoice. Do you realize what happened?

It's this simple transaction. There's nothing wrong, that's how businesses work. Dozens or hundreds of transactions are made a year that way.

I ask you what happens if your client does not pay you the USD 700 after 30 days?

Well, the answer is obvious, you will have to take out of your cash and pay to your supplier and you will have a negative cash of USD 500 momentarily. What, if another customer wants to buy you another bike? Where you will get the $ 300 to pay to your supplier?

You have to go to the bank or friend and they will lend you $ 300, but the rates are probably high and if you stop selling, the result is that you lose market share because you ran out of capital.

However, in your accounting you have an invoice (Sale) of USD 700. But it was not charged (This is one of the accounting traps)

5.4 Why companies go bankrupt

I think you already figured it out. But I reinforce it.

Entrepreneurs only look at the profit and loss statement, but that is "fictitious." The real thing is CASH. So companies go bankrupt for a single reason, they ran out of cash and have no sources of financing, their employees will not wait for their client to pay, there will be discontent, the work environment declines, and everything becomes a small disaster, that happens with the small, medium and large companies, and it causes bankruptcies. You can have the best "clients" but you don't know if this client got into trouble and also ran out of cash. This problem is super classic, it has happened with the largest companies such as General Electric and many more.

And the only thing managers do when the subject gets complex:
a. Cut staff
b. Wages drop
C. They reduce travel expenses
d. Other more extreme measures such as selling the business

All due to poor management of the conditions of sale and customer evaluation and you will hear this phrase, Net Working Capital is now our priority.

Always having a negative NWC is ideal. I have seen this problem in all the companies where I have worked.

Managers immediately will try to correct the situation by sending an email to all employees, saying that from now, we do not make sales without cash in advance, and we pay suppliers with invoices within 60 days, but it is not so easy anymore.

Most managers have bonus packages for sales and not for cash flow generation, so they push the sales team to sell, sell !! creating an insane situation.

There are hundreds of companies that go bankrupt due to poor cash flow management, do not forget this, it is better to sell little, always ensuring your cash generation.

5.5 Why companies are successful and sustainable
After an exhaustive study of successful cases of companies in the world and from my own experience, we are going to list them.

A. Leadership level 5: Humility + Will

The level 5 leader is one who combines extraordinary personal humility and a strong professional will" and defines them as those who "divert their selfish needs from themselves and channel them towards a larger goal of creating a great company. Of course they have personal interests; in fact, they are incredibly ambitious, but their ambition is above all for their institution, not for themselves

B. Who first? And that?

The main point is that you have to first get competent people and get the incompetent off the bus, and only then think about where to go. Absolute rigor is required in decisions to take the company from good to outstanding.

The rigor in prominent companies is applied first to those at the top, to those with greater responsibilities.

➢ Golden rule # 1. When in doubt, don't hire, keep looking.

➢ Golden rule # 2. When you need to change people, take action.

➢ Golden rule # 3. Dedicate the best people to the big opportunities, not the big problems.

C. Face the facts naked. Facing adverse events without giving up and with discipline. The decisive results are the consequence of good decisions, executed with diligence and accumulated one on top of the other". But I clarify that: "In no way is it possible to make a series of good decisions without first facing the naked facts. "Facts are better than dreams"

Basic practices for the truth to be heard:
➢ Lead with questions, not answers.
➢ Use dialogue and debate, not coercion.
➢ Perform autopsies without blaming anyone.
➢ Create alert mechanisms.

D. Hedgehog concept. They are not based on competition but on the three intersecting circles. The Greek fable "The hedgehog and the fox" points out that the fox knows many things, but the hedgehog knows one very great thing. The comparison of some people with foxes, who pursue many goals at the same time and see the world in all its complexity, are scattered and diffuse and move on many levels, without ever integrating their ideas into a single unifying concept". But he also talks about the Comparison of some people with hedgehogs, which simplify a complex world into a single organizing idea, a basic principle that unifies and guides everything. However, complex the world is, however, the hedgehog reduces all challenges and dilemmas to simple ideas. For a hedgehog, everything that is not related in some way to the idea of him is irrelevant. The strategic difference is based on:

First Circle: Outstanding companies base their strategy on a deep understanding of three dimensions (three circles).

Second Circle: They translate that understanding into a simple, crystalline concept that guides them in all their endeavors.
First circle: in which I can be the best in the world;
second circle: what drives its economic engine.

Third circle: What you are passionate about. The companies that never came out from good to outstanding were as follows: First, the right questions outlined in the three circles were never asked. Second, they set their goals and strategies more out of bragging than understanding. Discipline culture. No hierarchy bureaucracy or control is required (discipline + employer = success).

Business success is fueled by creativity, imagination and daring forays into unknown fields", but it is necessary: "to create a culture of individuals who act in a disciplined manner within the three circles rigidly consistent with the hedgehog concept. "" The secret of going from good to excellent lies largely in the discipline to do whatever it takes to become the best in carefully selected areas, and then to seek continual improvement. It's that easy. Discipline is essential for optimal results, but disciplined action without sticking to all three circles cannot lead to great sustained results. Featured companies follow a simple slogan: We will not do anything that does not conform to our hedgehog concept. We will not engage in business that is not related to him. We won't make acquisitions or partner with others in business if they don't fit in, we won't.

F. Technology accelerators

They don't use it as a primary means of transformation, but they understand its importance. Becoming a large company is discovering how to apply technology to a coherent concept that reflects the understanding of the three circles. From the good to the outstanding, we find technological sophistication, applying carefully selected new technologies. Technology is paramount, but only after he discovered his hedgehog concept and after achieving decisive results. " Well, she: "is key to transformation and acts as an accelerating factor. To determine if technology is beneficial in the transition it is necessary to ask the following questions:

- ➢ It fits directly into her hedgehog concept.
- ➢ Is this technology really needed? If the answer is yes, then one has to pioneer its application.

Warren Edward Buffett (Omaha, Nebraska, August 30, 1930) is an American investor and businessman. He is considered one of the largest investors in the world, as well as being the largest shareholder and Chairman and CEO of Berkshire Hathaway. Known as the "Oracle of Omaha"

His investment style is as follows.

1. Buy only simple and understandable companies that he understands.

2. Companies with a favorable operating history. For Buffet, the best returns are obtained by companies that have been producing the same product or service for several years. Making changes in large companies increases the probability of making mistakes in large companies.

3. Favorable long-term prospects.
According to Buffet, companies are divided into two groups:

I. A small group of franchises.
II. A much larger group of core businesses.
Defines a Franchise as a company that provides a product or service that does not have a similar substitute and is not regulated. This allows you to increase product prices without losing market share.

On the contrary, the basic business company offers a product practically indistinguishable from its competitors, years ago the basic products were gasoline, chemicals, wheat, copper, wood. Today it is computers, cars, airlines, banks and insurance that have become merchandise.

4. Rationality

I. In the development phase, a company loses money when it develops products and establishes a market.

II. In the next phase of rapid growth, the company is profitable, but growing so fast that it cannot support growth, it often has to not only retain all its earnings but also have to borrow money or issue stocks for financial growth.

III. In the third phase of maturity, the growth rate slows and the company begins to generate more money than it needs to develop and cover its costs.

IV. In the last phase, the decline phase, the company suffers a decline in sales and profits, but continues to generate excess money.

It is in phase three and four, but especially in phase three that the question arises, how should these benefits be distributed? If the extra money, when reinvested internally, can produce an above-average return on capital, a return that is slightly above the cost of capital, the company should retain all of its profits and reinvest them. It is the only logical thing. If the opposite happens, we already know what the obvious answer is.

Bibliography

1. How has covid-19 affected local entrepreneurs? Sept 01, 2020 - Care.
2. Why do companies fail? - Lar organizations during the Covid 19, Sept 17, 2020 - Dr. Pinkas Flink.
3. Why do organizations fail? Alcides Zenteno.
4. Business Valuation and Financial Reports - Prof. Eduardo Pablo - 2010 - Tulane University.
5. Why project financial statements? - Prof. Eduardo Pablo - 2010 - Tulane University.
6. The top-down approach - Prof. Eduardo Pablo - 2010 - Tulane -University.
7. What is the cost of Capital Opportunity? - Prof. Eduardo Pablo - 2010 - Tulane University.
8. 10 companies that failed to innovate, resulting in business failure - Frances Goh - She is an innovation consultant, brand strategist and customer champion.
9. 10 Successful American Businesses That Have Failed Overseas - American business international business on September12,2013.
10. Business Adventures - Twelve Classic Wall Street Tales - John Brooks - 1969.
11. The Money Traps - Dan Ariely and Jeff Kreisler April 2018.
12. Small Business Administration - Pierina del Refuge nuño de León - 2012.
13. Typical causes of failure - Jaime Cavero - President of the Mentor Day Accelerator -2019.
14. Companies or myths? Common elements of the oldest companies in the world The importance of demystification - Hugo Alberto Rivera Rodríguez - October 2006.

15. productivity and competitiveness in Quindío: an analysis from the perspective of the competitive advantage of nations by Michael Porter Ivis I. Salas and Juliana Hurtado -2014
16. 46% of companies in the region obtain results in digital transformation - Sergio Mavila, from InterNexa World - Oct 2020.
17. Companies That Excel Why Some Can I improve Profitability and others Can't - Jim Collins 2007.
18. The Competitive Advantage according to Michael Porter - 1980 Harvard Professor.
19. Warren Buffet - Strategies from the Investor Who Turned $ 100 Into $ 14 Billion - Robert G. Hagstrom Jr. - 1999.
20. Berkshire Hathaway Letters to Shareholders 1965 -2014 Warren Buffett and Max Olson - 2016.
21. Winning - Jack Welch and Suzy Welch - April 2006
22. Impact of financing plans on SMEs during the Pandemic - Walther Reátegui Vela Professor at ESAN - Sept 2020.
23. Implementing Value Based Management - Samuel C. Weaver College of Business and Economics Lehigh University - June 3, 2003.
24. Value Maximization, Stakeholder Theory, and the Corporate Objective Function - Michael C. Jensen - The Monitor Group and Harvard Business School - February 13, 2001.
25. Definitive Jack - (straight from the gut) Jack Welch, John Byrne - 2001
26. The Innovators: How a Group of Hackers, Geniuses, and Geeks Created the Digital Revolution - Los Innovators the Geniuses Who invented the Future Walter Isaacson, 2014.

27. The Innovator's Dilemma - When New Technologies Fail Big Firms Harvard Business School Press, 1997 Clayton M. Christensen
28. The Rise and Fall of General Electric (GE) - Sarah Hansen Updated, Mar 26, 2020.

www.ingramcontent.com/pod-product-compliance
Lightning Source LLC
Chambersburg PA
CBHW050322220526
45465CB00005B/2088